Maritimes

Jessica Morrison

Weigl

Published by Weigl Educational Publishers Limited
6325 10th Street SE
Calgary, Alberta, Canada T2H 2Z9

Website: www.weigl.com

Library and Archives Canada Cataloguing in Publication

Morrison, J. A. (Jessica A.), 1984-
        Maritimes / Jessica Morrison.
(Canadian ecozones)
Includes index.
Also available in electronic format.
ISBN 978-1-55388-637-2 (bound).--ISBN 978-1-55388-638-9 (pbk.)
        1. Natural history--Maritime Provinces--Juvenile literature.
2. Ecology--Maritime Provinces--Juvenile literature. 3. Occupations--
Maritime Provinces--Juvenile literature. 4. Ecological zones--Maritime
Provinces--Juvenile literature. 5. Maritime Provinces--Juvenile literature.
I. Title. II. Series: Canadian ecozones

QH106.2.M37M67 2010   j577.09715   C2009-907303-X

Printed in the United States of America in North Mankato, Minnesota
1 2 3 4 5 6 7 8 9 0 14 13 12 11 10

072010
WEP230610

Project Coordinator
Heather Kissock

Designers
Warren Clark, Janine Vangool

Photograph Credits

Weigl acknowledges Getty Images as its primary image supplier for this title.

Every reasonable effort has been made to trace ownership and to obtain permission to reprint copyright material. The publishers would be pleased to have any errors or omissions brought to their attention so that they may be corrected in subsequent printings.

We acknowledge the financial support of the Government of Canada through the Canada Book Fund for our publishing activities.

CONTENTS

Introduction

Canada is one of the largest countries in the world and also one of the most diverse. It spans nearly 10 million square kilometres, from the Pacific Ocean in the west to the Atlantic Ocean in the east. Canada's vast landscape features a wide range of geography. Yet, as diverse as the country's geography is, some areas still share common characteristics. These regions are called ecozones. Along with common geographic features, ecozones share similar climates and life forms, such as plants and animals.

Ecozones demonstrate the reliance between **organisms** and their environment. All organisms have unique survival needs. Some organisms thrive in cold, while others require hot climates. They rely on their environment to meet their needs. Just like a puzzle, every organism has its own place in an ecozone.

The rugged coastline of British Columbia's Cape Scott Provincial Park is characteristic of a maritime ecozone.

Canada has both terrestrial, or land-based, and marine, or water-based, ecozones. The terrestrial ecozones can be grouped into five broad categories. These are Arctic, shields, plains, maritimes, and cordilleras.

Canada's maritime ecozones are some of the most unique landscapes in the world. The combination of ocean and land creates incredible **habitats** for different species of plants and animals. The Pacific Maritime ecozone borders the Pacific Ocean, while the Atlantic Maritime ecozone runs alongside the Atlantic Ocean. Although these areas are separated by the huge landmass of Canada, they are similar in many ways.

Many plants and animals have **adapted** to survive in the maritime ecozones. As they are located close to water, many organisms have also developed ways of making use of this large resource.

FASCINATING FACTS

Canada has more than 243,000 kilometres of coastline. This is more than any other country in the world.

The Pacific Ocean is the biggest ocean in the world. It covers almost 33 percent of Earth's surface. The Atlantic Ocean is the world's second-largest ocean.

Maritime Locations

s their name suggests, maritime ecozones are situated close to major bodies of water. The Pacific and Atlantic Maritime ecozones are located on opposite sides of Canada, near the oceans that match their names.

The Pacific Maritime ecozone is on the western coast of Canada. It covers more than 195,000 square kilometres and includes the Coast Mountains, British Columbia's marine islands, and the southwest corner of the Yukon Territory. The ecozone also includes 900 square kilometres of shoreline. The Pacific Maritime ecozone is within what is called the "Ring of Fire." This is a large, semi-circular area on the planet that is known for active volcanoes, hot springs, and earthquakes.

The Coast Mountains run almost the entire length of the Pacific Maritime ecozone, from the Yukon to southern British Columbia.

Percé Rock is one of the most identifiable landmarks of the Gaspé Peninsula. It features one of the world's largest natural arches.

The Atlantic Maritime ecozone is located on the eastern side of Canada. It has a diverse landscape, spanning from the Gaspé Peninsula to the Maritime Provinces. Prince Edward Island, Nova Scotia, and New Brunswick are all part of this ecozone. More than three quarters of the Atlantic Maritime ecozone is covered with forests.

FASCINATING FACTS

The Atlantic Maritime ecozone covers about two percent of Canada's total land area.

About 11,200 kilometres of shoreline form the outline of the Atlantic Maritime ecozone.

Mount Logan, Canada's highest mountain, is located in the Pacific Maritime ecozone. It stands at 5,959 metres.

British Columbia's Coast Mountains extend 1,600 kilometres north to south. Their widest point spans 200 kilometres. Mount Waddington, British Columbia's highest peak, is located within this mountain range. It stands at 4,016 metres tall.

CANADA'S ECOZONES

Canada has five major ecozone categories. Like the maritimes, however, these categories can be broken down into specific ecozones. The inset map shows where these ecozones are located.

Look closely at the map of the maritime ecozones. Besides oceans, what other features do maritime ecozones appear to have?

Pacific Maritime

Montane Cordillera

Boreal Cordillera

Taiga Cordillera

Taiga Plains

Boreal Plains

Hudson Plains

Prairie

Taiga Shield

Boreal Shield

Mixedwood Plains

Atlantic Maritime

Southern Arctic

Northern Arctic

Arctic Cordillera

United States

Yukon

Mount Logan

Pacific Ocean

Coast Mountains

British Columbia

Prince Rupert

Haida Gwaii
Banks Island — Pitt Island

Queen Charlotte Strait

Rivers Inlet

Knight Inlet

Brooks Peninsula

Mount Waddington

Vancouver Island

Malaspina Peninsula

Georgia Strait

Gulf Islands

Vancouver

Mount Garibaldi

Burrard Peninsula

Cascade Range

Victoria

Saanich Peninsula

N

0   500 kilometres

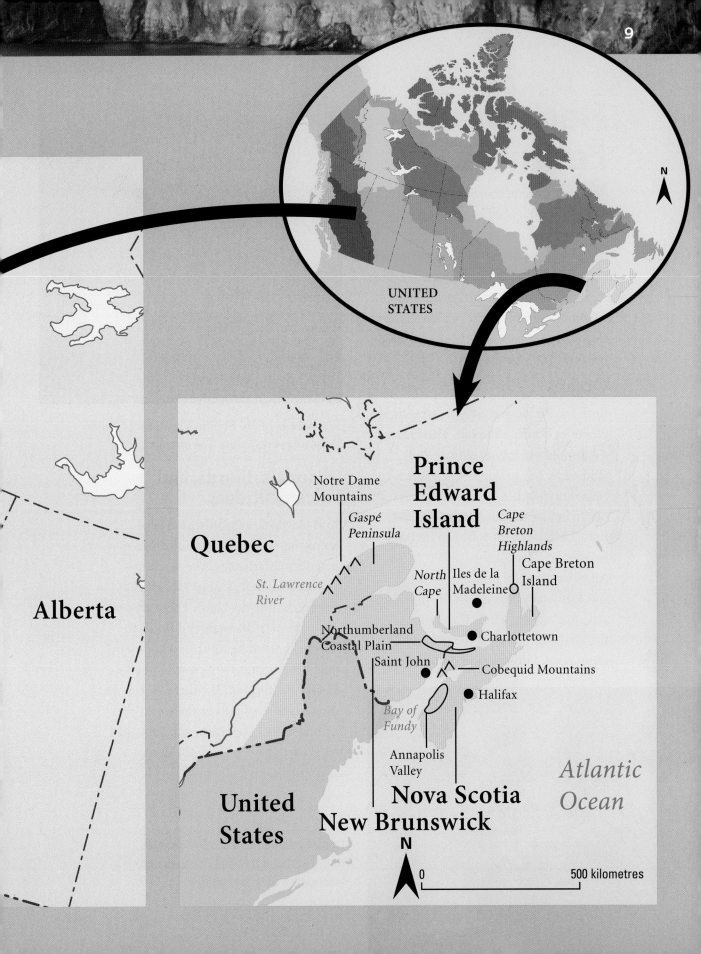

N

UNITED
STATES

Alberta

Notre Dame
Mountains

*Gaspé
Peninsula*

Prince
Edward
Island

*Cape
Breton
Highlands*

Quebec

*St. Lawrence
River*

*North
Cape*

Iles de la
Madeleine

Cape Breton
Island

Northumberland
Coastal Plain

Charlottetown

Saint John

Cobequid Mountains

Halifax

*Bay of
Fundy*

*Atlantic
Ocean*

Annapolis
Valley

Nova Scotia

United
States

New Brunswick

N

0   500 kilometres

Maritime Features

Maritime ecozones are greatly influenced by their primary feature—oceans. In fact, nearby oceans have had a major impact on many of the landforms found in the maritime ecozones. The Pacific and Atlantic Maritime ecozones have many **fjords**, mountains, forests, peninsulas, beaches, and islands.

Oceans

Both the Pacific and Atlantic Maritime ecozones border an ocean. This creates a constantly changing climate and landscape. Ocean winds cause waves to rush onto beaches. **Erosion** is constantly occurring in maritime ecozones. Over time, large pieces of rock can become smaller boulders, stones, and pebbles. All of the sand on maritime beaches was formed by erosion. In the maritime ecozones, strong winds travel over the landscape, eroding the surfaces of mountains, hillsides, and dunes.

The islands of the Pacific Maritime ecozone feature several inlets and channels.

Channels, Fjords, and Volcanic Ridges

Both maritime ecozones have very interesting and unique landforms. In the Pacific Maritime ecozone, deep **channels**, as well as steep mountains and fjords, line the coast. These are some of the deepest channels and fjords in the world, running up to 190 kilometres long. Both features are created when glaciers cut through the surface of Earth. The deepest channels in the world are formed in this way. Although some of the glaciers have melted, the deep cuts remain.

Ocean waters have eroded coastal rocks in the maritime ecozones, making interesting rock formations.

The tip of the Gaspé Peninsula can be seen from a viewing platform at Cap Bon-Ami.

Peninsulas

A peninsula is a piece of land that is almost completely surrounded by water. It is connected to the mainland by a small bit of land called an isthmus. In the Pacific Maritime ecozone, the Burrard Peninsula, Malaspina Peninsula, and Saanich Peninsula are popular tourist attractions. In the Atlantic Maritime ecozone, there are peninsulas in New Brunswick and Nova Scotia. Some of the oldest settlements of the Atlantic Maritimes are found on these peninsulas. Since peninsulas are much like islands, they share many of the same climatic and environmental features.

FASCINATING FACTS

The Pacific Maritime ecozone is home to a temperate rain forest. This type of rain forest is found along the sea coast in warm regions of the world. It receives moisture from a combination of rain and fog.

Forests cover about 50 percent of the Pacific Maritime ecozone.

The Atlantic Maritime ecozone is known for its many large, stacked rock formations known as sea stacks. These towering formations were created very slowly 600 million to 13,000 years ago.

Climate in the Maritimes

Even though the climates in the Pacific and Atlantic Maritime ecozones differ from each other, they share some similarities. This is because they are both located close to large oceans. The Pacific Ocean impacts the climate of the Pacific Maritime ecozone, while the Atlantic Ocean affects the Atlantic Maritime ecozone. In general, oceans can bring storms, wind, and precipitation to a region.

Wet Weather in the West

The Pacific Maritime ecozone has the wettest weather in Canada. Coastal areas can receive up to 4,000 millimetres of precipitation each year. This is

The Pacific Ocean sends strong winds toward the land. This means the weather can be very different from day to day.

because the large mountains stop the precipitation from reaching farther inland. As a result, this region is one of the most humid, with moisture clinging to the air much of the time. Farther inland, in the Georgia Strait region, levels of precipitation are much lower, roughly 600 millimetres each year. The temperature in most areas of Canada changes substantially from summer to winter. However, in the Pacific Maritime ecozone, there is little change between monthly temperatures. In July, the average temperature ranges between 12 and 18 degrees Celsius. In the winter months, temperatures average around −1.5 degrees Celsius.

Atlantic Influence

Cool summers and warm winters occur in the Atlantic Maritimes, with roughly 900 millimetres of precipitation each year. In those areas closest to the coast, the amount of precipitation can reach more than 1,500 millimetres a year. Due to this precipitation, this ecozone has more storms than any other in Canada. The region also receives the second highest annual precipitation. In the winter, the average temperature is −5 degrees Celsius. Summers in this area average 14 to 18 degrees Celsius.

Fog and the Labrador Current

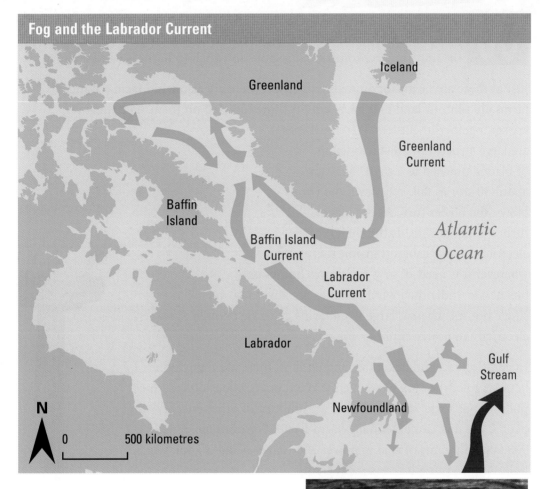

In the Atlantic Maritime ecozone, fog blankets much of the landscape in late spring and early summer. This is due to the Gulf Stream mixing with the Labrador Current. The Gulf Stream is a warm flow of water, and the Labrador Current is cold. This combination of warm and cold makes fog.

FASCINATING FACTS

The wettest and cloudiest town in Canada is Prince Rupert, located on British Columbia's northwest coast. This region has received 2,552 millimetres of precipitation in one year.

Frost is common in the Atlantic Maritime ecozone. There are only 80 frost-free days in New Brunswick each year.

Technology in the Maritimes

Wind energy is one of the latest innovations in the **green movement**. Wind is a free and potentially endless resource. Winds coming off the oceans make the maritime ecozones great regions in which to harness wind energy.

Just as there are farms for animals and crops, there are also wind farms. Wind farms are plots of land that have wind turbines erected on them. The turbines are set together in clusters. Wind turbines are large structures, most consisting of blades attached to a shaft. They are about 30 stories tall. Whenever the wind blows, the blades turn. As the blades turn, a generator inside the shaft creates electricity. Large cables transmit this energy wherever it is needed, so it can power homes and businesses. Individual wind turbines are able to power single homes, whereas large wind farms generate enough electricity to power entire towns.

In addition to wind being free and endless, there are many other benefits to harnessing wind energy. Wind energy does not produce pollution or toxic waste. It lowers the amount of other energy sources people use that can potentially harm Earth. For example, it takes 900,000 kilograms of coal to power 200 homes. Coal is a known pollutant. Burning it releases dangerous **greenhouse gases** into the air. If wind energy is used to power 200 homes, greenhouse gas emissions can be lowered by 2,000 tonnes. This is equivalent to planting 10,000 trees. Wind energy also helps to conserve water, a vital resource on the planet. Apart from using a small amount of water to wipe down the blades, wind turbines require no water to function.

A large wind turbine can produce enough electricity to power about 600 homes.

The North Cape Wind Farm was constructed in two phases. It was completed in 2003.

In the Atlantic Maritime ecozone, there are more than 25 large-scale wind farms in operation. One of the largest, Kent Hills, is located in New Brunswick. Another large wind farm, the North Cape Wind Farm, is located in Prince Edward Island. The North Cape Wind Farm contains 16 wind turbines, which is enough to power 4,000 houses. In total, the wind farms of Canada create enough electricity to power about one million homes.

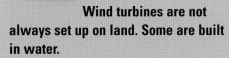

FASCINATING FACTS

Wind is a renewable resource. It is, and always will be, available to use. Coal is a non-renewable resource. Once it is used, it is gone forever.

All of the wind in the world is powered by the Sun. When the Sun shines on Earth, it heats the land to different temperatures in different places. Warm air rises, and cooler air descends, moving from high pressure to low pressure systems. The constant shifting of air is wind.

Wind turbines are not always set up on land. Some are built in water.

LIFE IN THE MARITIMES

The Atlantic and Pacific Maritime ecozones are full of unique and interesting organisms. Since the maritimes are found at the coastlines of Canada, they are home to many terrestrial and marine species.

The Puget Sound king crab is one of the largest crabs on the Pacific coast.

INVERTEBRATES

Animals with no backbones, or invertebrates, represent a large portion of all the animals on Earth. Some invertebrates live on land and others live in oceans, lakes, and rivers. Invertebrates use special methods to catch food. Crabs living along maritime coasts **scavenge** or actively hunt their food. Oysters are called filter feeders because they filter suspended **plankton** from the water. Small, hair-like structures called cilia capture microscopic food particles.

AMPHIBIANS

In order to survive, amphibians must keep their skin wet or moist at all times. Many amphibians live in the maritime ecozones because they are moist environments. The Pacific giant salamander is just one of the many species of salamanders that live in the Pacific Maritime ecozone. The Atlantic Maritime region also has five species of salamanders and newts. Salamanders, like most amphibians, lay their eggs in water.

The Pacific giant salamander can reach lengths up to 30 centimetres.

Many birds build their nests along the shores and trees of the maritime coastlines.

BIRDS

Birds have many adaptations to help them survive in the maritime coastal environments. **Predatory** birds, such as bald eagles, have sharp eyesight and talons. This enables them to hunt reptiles, fish, and other birds. Some maritime birds, such as ducks and geese, spend much of their time in the water. They also spend a great deal of time **preening**. This helps their feathers stay waterproof and warm.

REPTILES

Reptiles cannot regulate their own body temperature, so they must stay in areas that are warm. To warm their bodies every morning, reptiles bask on rocks or in open areas. This is why it is most common to see reptiles at the break of day. Most reptiles are terrestrial. However, the Atlantic Maritime ecozone is home to several marine turtles, including the loggerhead and the **endangered** leatherback. The leatherback turtle can also be found in the Pacific Maritime ecozone.

PLANTS

The plants found in the Pacific and Atlantic Maritime ecozones are diverse. Some plants, such as marram grass, grow close to the water, peeking out between rocks and crevasses. Larger plants, such as red cedar trees, form some of the largest forests in the world. All plants need different amounts of water, sunlight, and **nutrients** to grow. Some plants have adapted to survive the salty ocean water sprays, while others can only live in areas with fresh water. To help it survive the varied climate of the Maritimes, each plant has unique adaptations.

An adult loggerhead turtle can weigh up to 454 kilograms.

Maritime Plants

Berry Bushes and Shrubs

The Pacific and Atlantic Maritime ecozones have different species of berry bushes and shrubs. These berries are a food source for birds and mammals. In the Pacific Maritimes, red elderberry, huckleberry, and salmonberry thrive. Blueberries and smooth juneberries are common to the Atlantic Maritime ecozone. Berries keep seeds safe and help to disperse them. Dispersal happens when animals eat the berries and drop the seeds in their **scat**. This helps young plants to grow in other areas.

Salmonberries look much like raspberries, but are more orange than red.

The most common grass in the Atlantic Maritime is marram grass. This grass helps to stabilize the ground, with strong roots that hold onto the soil.

Marsh Grasses and Plants

Several plants live in the **intertidal zone** of the Atlantic Maritime ecozone. This area is very harsh, with icy cold water and strong, hot winds. Salt marsh grasses are plants that can survive the salty water and strong winds of the intertidal zone. They can do this because they have special adaptations. To avoid becoming waterlogged, salt marsh grasses have hollow ducts in their stems. This allows air to move to the roots, where it is most needed. These grasses are also flexible and tough. This helps them bend with the wind and currents of the intertidal zone. In the Pacific Maritime ecozone, cattails can withstand the extreme climate because they have deep roots called rhizomes. Rhizomes grow quickly. This allows the cattails to root themselves to the wet earth before the wind carries them away.

Trees

The trees of the Pacific Maritime ecozone are some of the largest and oldest in the world. Some trees, such as the Douglas fir, grow to 80 metres high and are 14 metres in diameter. Others, such as the Sitka Spruce, can reach more than 90 metres tall. These trees grow to amazing heights because of the warm, moist climate of the Pacific Maritimes. The Atlantic Maritimes also have numerous forests. Spruce, maple, and fir are the most common trees found there. All trees have unique systems to help them transport water and nutrients to their highest leaves. Deep inside the tree is a series of channels. These channels, or tubes, are called **xylem** and **phloem**. Xylem channels are used to pull the water all the way to the top of the tree. Phloem channels transport nutrients to different parts of the tree. Together, these two channels make sure that even the tallest trees receive the energy and water they need to continue growing.

There are 150 known species of maple trees in the world. Only 10 of these species are found in Canada.

FASCINATING FACTS

Some of the red cedar trees of the Pacific Maritime ecozone live to be more than 800 years old. These trees were often used by Aboriginal Peoples for building canoes and totem poles.

Saltwater can be damaging to plants. This is because the salt in the water can disrupt the balance of water in the plant cells. In the Atlantic Maritimes, white spruce can tolerate salt water. This is a unique adaptation that enables it to survive near the coast.

Birds, Mammals, and Fish

Birds

Birds are common in the maritime ecozones. Tufted puffins are **pelagic** birds of the Pacific coast. This means they spend much of their time near open water. Puffins feed on fish and invertebrates. They have special spines inside their mouths that help them hold onto many fish at one time. The American black oystercatcher is another Pacific shorebird. It has a bright red bill and pink legs. These birds use their sharp bills to pick up food items, such as mussels, oysters, and clams. In the Atlantic Maritime ecozone, the great blue heron stalks its prey with its long, skinny legs. Herons move so slowly in the water that small fish do not know they are in danger. Herons then use their long beaks to capture fish one at a time. The piping plover is another shorebird in Atlantic Canada. Plovers are sand-coloured, which helps them blend into their environment and avoid predators.

A single porcupine can have more than 30,000 quills. It will lose about 700 during an attack.

Mammals

Mammals have found many ways to thrive in the maritime ecozones. In the Pacific Maritime ecozone, omnivores, such as black bears, survive by eating almost anything they can find. Berries, meat, roots, shoots, and fish are all part of a black bear's diet. The sea otter is another mammal that survives near the coastline. These animals can swim well, which allows them to spend time on land and in the water. In the Atlantic Maritime ecozone, porcupines are common. Porcupines have hard, sharp quills that bristle when the animal is in danger.

Tufted puffins are social animals. They live in large groups called colonies.

Sockeye salmon are known for their bright red skin.

Fish

There are many species of fish in the maritime ecozones. Some fish live in salt water, while others live in fresh water. Some fish can even survive in both environments. Several species of salmon live in the Pacific and Atlantic Maritime ecozones. Many of these salmon return to the same river they were hatched from to **spawn**. Salmon have adapted a unique way of ensuring the survival of their young. They do not take care of them. Instead, they lay hundreds of eggs. Some of these eggs will be eaten by predators. However, due to the number of eggs, it is likely that many will grow to become adult salmon. Many other types of fish and amphibians use this same strategy.

FASCINATING FACTS

Black bears are not always black. Black bears can be brown, cinnamon, or even white.

Sea otters are some of the furriest animals in the world. To protect them from cold waters, every square centimetre of their fur has up to 100,000 hairs.

Bird feathers are used as insulators. They protect the bird from cool wind and rain.

Killer whales are mammals found in the Pacific Maritime waters. Although they live in the water, whales need oxygen to survive. They have blowholes on the top of their head to help them breathe oxygen when they come to the surface of the water. When a whale surfaces, it exhales quickly. The whale then inhales before it dives back into the water.

Invertebrates, Amphibians, and Reptiles

Sea slugs, a type of invertebrate, can often be found attached to kelp and other ocean plants.

Invertebrates

Crustaceans are common in the maritime ecozones. A crustacean is a type of invertebrate. Crabs, lobsters, shrimps, and barnacles are all crustaceans. Many crustaceans use feathery legs, called cirri, to sweep through the water and collect small food particles. Most crustaceans feed on plankton, another type of invertebrate. There are two main kinds of plankton. Zooplankton are single-celled animals that feed on other plankton. Phytoplankton live near the surface of the water, and make their own food through a process called **photosynthesis**. This is the same process that plants on land use to survive. As they are plentiful, plankton are an important food source for many animals in maritime waters.

Amphibians

In the Pacific Maritime ecozone, the moist environment is perfect for amphibians. Pacific tree frogs hide under logs and leaves, using their sticky toe pads to climb and search for their food. The western toad stays near quiet, standing water and other damp areas. When they are not hunting for insects, these toads stay underground in burrows beneath rocks and logs. In the Atlantic Maritimes, the yellow-spotted salamander is very common in areas with ponds. It eats worms and spiders. To avoid being eaten by predators, the yellow-spotted salamander stays in burrows or under logs most of the time.

Pacific tree frogs change their colour with the temperature. On warm days, they are light green. On cold days, they are dark green.

The Atlantic Ridley turtle is also known as the Kemp's Ridley. It was named after the fisher who first found it.

Reptiles

Sharptail snakes are one type of reptile that lives in the Pacific Maritimes. These snakes lay their eggs in late spring, in a large group with other sharptail snake eggs. When the baby snakes hatch out of their eggs, they are fully developed. This helps them to start hunting right away. In the Atlantic Maritimes, marine turtles live in the ocean waters. The Atlantic Ridley sea turtle is the smallest of all sea turtles and the most endangered. It has a large, heart-shaped shell and eats crabs, jellyfish, squid, and snails.

FASCINATING FACTS

The bottom of a turtle shell is known as a plastron. The top is called a carapace.

The word plankton comes from the greek work *planktos*, which means "wanderer."

Some animals make their homes on other animals. Barnacles are often seen on the backs and fins of large whales.

Maritimes in Danger

The Pacific and Atlantic Maritime ecozones are some of the most stunning parts of Canada. However, these areas suffer from many environmental threats.

As there are many marine animals and plants in these regions, ocean pollution becomes a serious problem. Plastics and other bits of garbage are eaten by birds and mammals, or get tangled up in the fins of sea turtles and fish. Animals may not be killed by the garbage, but they can get injured by plastic cords and netting.

Maritime ecozones are also in danger from the arrival of plants and animals that are not **indigenous** to the area. Species that take over an area and push other organisms out are known as invasive. The various **ecosystems** within an ecozone are delicate, and new species can interrupt the balance between the area's indigenous plants and animals. When a new species invades an ecosystem, it takes nutrients and space from other organisms.

Invasive species are often brought to an area by humans. Many invasive species arrive on boats.

Besides removing habitat, the logging industry also pollutes the air with toxins.

In the Pacific Maritimes, logging and other forest industries are common. They are also important for the economic growth of the province. However, logging impacts the landscape. More than two million hectares of coastal forest have been clear-cut in the past 120 years. This means most of the trees in an area were completely removed all at once. Trees are habitats for many animals. When they are removed, animals lose their homes. Deep tree roots also help to prevent erosion by holding soil in place across the forest. Removing trees can result in looser soil, which can cause landscapes to wash away.

FASCINATING FACTS

Fish farming is a major source of income for many coastal communities. However, a great deal of seafood has become contaminated with toxins. Many of these pollutants are a result of human actions.

The bullfrog is native to southeastern Canada, but it is an invasive species in British Columbia. Their huge appetite has led to the decline of many of the area's native reptiles and amphibians, including the red-legged frog.

WORKING IN THE MARITIMES

People who study the maritime ecozones are knowledgeable in the areas of science, conservation, and ecology. They often enjoy the water and can handle extremes in weather.

MARINE BIOLOGIST

- Duties: collects and analyzes data about wildlife found in salt and fresh water

- Education: bachelor of science degree, specializing in marine biology or zoology

- Interests: zoology, chemistry, laboratory work, conservation, ecology

Marine biologists study underwater life, including species of fish, mammals, and invertebrates. They collect data and samples from the oceans, rivers, and lakes and help to plan conservation initiatives. Most marine biologists enjoy spending time on the water and have boating and scuba diving licences.

ECOLOGIST

- Duties: studies the relationship of living things to each other and to their environments

- Education: bachelor's, master's, or doctoral degree in environmental science or biology

- Interests: animal behaviour, animal and plant communities, how ecosystems work, environmental issues

Ecologists specialize in animals or plants and their interactions. Ecologists examine endangered species or ecosystems. They study the effects of pollution and develop species recovery plans. Some study soils or climate.

ENVIRONMENTAL SCIENTIST

- Duties: studies environments and determines ways to protect them

- Education: bachelor of science degree

- Interests: conservation, chemistry, biology

Environmental scientists work to ensure the planet is clean by studying the air, land, and water. Some environmental scientists specialize in chemistry. Environmental chemists help find out if certain chemicals are harmful to the environment. Other environmental scientists focus on protecting different animal and plant species.

ECO CHALLENGE

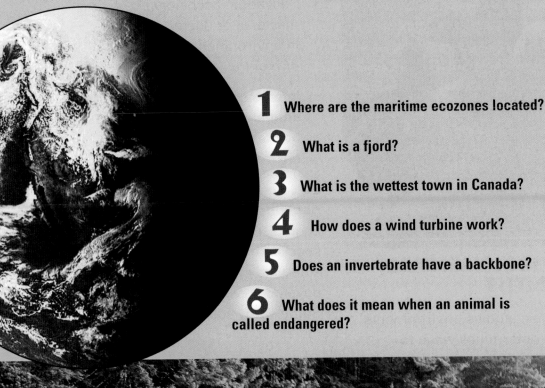

1 Where are the maritime ecozones located?

2 What is a fjord?

3 What is the wettest town in Canada?

4 How does a wind turbine work?

5 Does an invertebrate have a backbone?

6 What does it mean when an animal is called endangered?

7 How do trees transport water and nutrients to their tops?

8 What is a pelagic bird?

9 What are two types of plankton?

10 What does a marine biologist do?

Answers

1. At the east and west coasts of Canada; British Columbia, and Quebec with the Maritime provinces
2. A deep inlet of the sea with steep slopes on either sides
3. Prince Rupert, British Columbia
4. Wind turbines collect wind energy, converting it into electrical energy.
5. No
6. There are not many left in nature, and they require protection.
7. Xylem channels are used for water transport; phloem channels are used for nutrient transport.
8. A bird that spends most of its time in open waters.
9. Zooplankton and phytoplankton
10. Analyzes and studies marine animals found in salt and fresh water.

HOW WINDY IS IT?

Turbines of all types are used to generate electricity using wind energy. In order to create electricity, the wind must have a speed of about 23 kilometres per hour. Is the wind in your backyard strong enough to produce electricity? Make an anemometer to find out.

MATERIALS

- scissors
- 2 strips of stiff cardboard about 46 centimetres long
- stapler
- push pin
- sharpened pencil with an eraser
- modelling clay
- 4 paper drinking cups
- marker

1. With the help of an adult, carefully cut the rolled edges off the paper cups to make them a lighter weight.

2. Colour the outside of one cup with a marker so you can tell it apart from the others.

3. Cross the cardboard strips to form a plus sign.

4. Staple one cup to each end of the cardboard strips. One or two staples per cup will work. Make sure the cups all face the same direction.

5. Using the push pin, attach the cardboard cross to the eraser end of a pencil.

6. Outside, place some modelling clay on the ground. Stick the sharpened end of the pencil into the clay, securing it so it stands up straight.

7. When a gust of wind comes, use a stopwatch to count the number of times the cups spin around in one minute. Use your marked cup as a guide. Multiply the number of times it spins by 60 to convert your wind speed into kilometres per hour. Test the wind speed at different times during the day. Which times are windiest?

FURTHER RESEARCH

How can I find more information about maritime ecozones, plants, and animals?

- The Internet is a great source of information for all of these topics and more.

- Bookstores and libraries have many interesting books about ecozones, plants, and animals.

- Science centres and outdoor education centres are great places to learn hands-on about ecozones, plants, and animals.

BOOKS

Berkenkamp, Lauri. *Discover the Oceans.* Nomad Press: 2009

Hooper, Roseanne. *Life in the Coastlines.* Topeka Bindery: 2002

Parker, Steve. *Seashore - Eyewitness Books - Discover In Close-up The Ecology Of The Plants & Animals That Inhabit The Coastlines Of Our World.* Knopf: 1989.

WEBSITES

Where can I learn more about Canada's ecozones?

Park Wardens
www.parkwardens.com

Where can I learn about the plants and animals of the maritime ecozones?

Atlantic Maritimes
http://canadianbiodiversity.
mcgill.ca/english/ecozones/
atlanticmaritime/
atlanticmaritime.htm

Where can I learn about ecology?

Kids Do Ecology
http://kids.nceas.ucsb.edu

GLOSSARY

adapted: changed over time to suit the environment

channels: bodies of water that join other bodies of waters

ecosystems: communities of living things sharing an environment

endangered: at risk of no longer living on Earth

erosion: the process of wearing away

fjords: long, narrow ocean inlets, surrounded by steep cliffs

greenhouse gases: atmospheric gases that can reflect heat from the Sun back to Earth

green movement: the actions of people wanting to protect the environment

habitats: the places in which animals live

indigenous: native to an area

insulators: items that hold warmth

intertidal zone: the area of land that is covered by water during high tide, and exposed to air during low tide

nutrients: substances that provide nourishment

organisms: all living things

pelagic: found in the open water, not along coastlines

phloem: tubes found in trees that help transport nutrients

photosynthesis: the process by which a plant combines sunlight, water, and carbon dioxide to create energy

plankton: small organisms found in fresh or salt waters

predatory: preying on other animals for survival

preening: when a bird cleans its feathers

scat: waste from an animal

scavenge: to search out and eat animal carcasses

spawn: to lay eggs

xylem: tubes found in trees that transport water

INDEX